# No More Christianese

*Replacing Religious Language with Everyday Words*

Doug Addison

NO MORE CHRISTIANESE:
REPLACING RELIGIOUS LANGUAGE WITH EVERYDAY WORDS
Copyright ©2004 Doug Addison
All rights reserved.

Published by Fruit-Bearer Publishing
A Branch of Candy's Creations
P.O. Box 777, Georgetown, DE 19947
(302) 856-6649 • Fax (302) 856-7742
fruitbearer.publishing@verizon.net
www.fruitbearer.com
Cover design by Lai-Kit Chan
Edited by Candy Abbott
Printed in the USA

All rights reserved. No part of this publication may be reproduced, stored in a retrieval system, or transmitted in any form or by any means—electronic, mechanical, photocopy, recording, or any other—except for brief quotations in printed reviews, without the prior permission of the publisher or author, except as provided by USA copyright law.

ISBN 1-886068-27-5

## TO ORDER THIS BOOK

Doug Addison
InLight Connection
P.O. Box 58038
Sherman Oaks, CA 91413

1-800-507-7853
www.dougaddison.com

# Behind the Scenes

I wrote this booklet in response to numerous requests from people who want to learn how to communicate with friends and family members who are not familiar with the Bible or Christianity. After leading outreach events for a number of years, I noticed that people are actually very open to talking more about God—particularly when we use language that does not sound religious. My hope is that this booklet will help you share God's love with people in a way that can be more easily received. Not everyone we encounter will be open to hearing about the message of Jesus, but if we are rejected then at least it will not be because of our language.

I want to thank everybody who submitted religious words and have helped us come up with new definitions. Special thanks to my wife Linda, Lisa-Anne Wooldridge, Phyllis Watson, and others for their input and help with writing and editing; and to Lai-Kit Chan for the cover design.

Blessings,

*Doug Addison*

Doug Addison

# No More Christianese

Have you ever talked with other people about your religious beliefs? If your experience has been similar to mine, then I am sure you have gotten accustomed to "the wall." People tend to put up a barrier or a wall of defense when it comes to talking about God. The sad part of this is that many of these individuals are hurting and could really use some encouragement but, for whatever reason, they are not able to receive what we are saying. Because of this, I have spent a great deal of time studying the subject of sharing God's love with others.

I had a radical encounter with Jesus in 1985 that changed my life forever. I had been involved in occult practice for a number of years. Then, through a process of ominous circumstances and strange events, I not only realized how much I needed God's love but I found out firsthand that God's power is greater than any other spiritual power in the universe. Since the time I came out of extreme darkness and experienced God's extreme light, I have wanted to share it with everyone. I soon found that not everyone wanted to hear what I had to say. Deep inside, I knew if a person could only let down their wall of defense long enough to allow God to show Himself to them they would change their minds about Christianity.

As God began to draw me to Himself, I honestly did not know exactly what to do next. I knew some Christians at work but had a difficult time relating to them. I noticed that, particularly when they got around other Christians, they used words that I did not understand. When I went to church for the first time and was contemplating a relationship with God, I had no idea that there was an entire church sub-culture. It was like an "insider club" where they all assumed I knew their special language and all the things they did in their worship services. Oftentimes, I felt left out and had to work at it in order to fit in.

I remember asking someone to explain a few things to me and was told that I could get more information if I visited the vestibule. I had no idea what the vestibule was, let alone where to find it! Later I found out that the vestibule was the church lobby.

Someone asked me if I had been sanctified. "I'm not sure," I replied. "Is that a required class to join this church?"

A lot of people talked about conviction. I had no idea that there were so many ex-cons in the church.

A guy came up and told me that God had spoken to him that day while he was in his prayer closet. I thought, "I don't have one of those, are we supposed to pray in a closet?"

Somehow Christians have developed an "insider language" with sayings and words that are not used in everyday life at work or in school. I have found that in order for us to communicate effectively with people about God, we must learn to speak in a way that people without a religious background can understand.

Then it happened to me. One day after being involved with a Christian church for a number of years, I found myself cut off and out of relationship with my friends who were not Christian. These were the people who needed God the most. I realized that I also had developed a "church vocabulary," and I was using words that people outside the church did not understand. I wanted to share this wonderful, life-changing message of Jesus but lacked the ability to communicate it in a way that those without a religious background could comprehend!

One of the biggest barriers for sharing God's love with others is our communication style. In Colossians 4:3-6, the Apostle Paul wrote, ". . . praying at the same time for us . . . in order that I may make it clear in the way I ought to speak. Conduct yourselves with wisdom toward outsiders, making the most of the opportunity. Let your speech always be with grace, seasoned, as it were, with salt, so that you may know how you should respond to each person" (NASB).

Paul was very attentive to how he communicated with outsiders and gave a word of warning to the early church about it, as well. Paul addresses this issue in 1 Corinthians 14:9-11, ". . . if you talk to people in a language they don't understand, how will they know what you mean? You might as well be talking to an empty room. There are so many different languages in the world, and all are excellent for those who understand them, but to me they mean nothing. I will not understand people who speak those languages, and they will not understand me" (NLT).

When we try to talk with someone who has no religious background and we use words and phrases that are religious lingo, we might as well be speaking in a foreign language to them. The Apostle Paul was very strategic in the way he spoke to those outside the church. He often spoke differently with each group of people he encountered (see 1 Corinthians 9:20-23).

Over the years, I have searched for new and creative ways to reach people with God's love. I have found that people are very open to talking about God, particularly when we use language that they can understand.

I have come to realize that our society has changed dramatically over the past few decades. Even though we live in a country that has a lot of churches and claims to have Christian values, a good number of people no longer have a memory of Christianity passed down fom the generation before them. As a result, many of the popular methods of sharing God's love are not as effective as they once were.

I have also found that there are a great number of people who don't have a relationship with Jesus or don't go to church because they have been turned off by Christianity. This may have come through having a negative experience with an over-zealous religious family member or from having been wounded by an experience with a legalistic Christian. Many of these people are familiar with Christian lingo because they may have attended church. Quite often, they can be put off by words from their past that sound religious. For them, hearing a few "Thees" and "Thous" and "Shalt nots" and "Thus saiths" is like getting salt thrown in their wounds.

C. S. Lewis, a Christian writer, spoke of people who have been exposed to just enough Christianity to immunize them against the genuine thing. This group is another reason to avoid speaking religious—not because they don't know what the words mean, but because they do. For many, being familiar with those terms might bring up negative emotions or hurt feelings from the past. For others, the implications may be lost on them because they've "heard it all before." If we say the same things to them using everyday language, they are more likely to listen and understand.

As we venture out in finding ways to reach people with God's love, it is necessary for us to understand the people we want to reach. Missionaries who go to foreign countries train for years, studying the culture, language, and religion. They learn the peoples' customs, how to interact with them, and even how to translate the Bible into their native dialect. If we are to reach people in our own culture who do not know God's love, we must take the task as seriously as the missionaries do. We must realize that we are all missionaries in our own neighborhoods.

Jesus spoke in the language of His day, using parables and metaphors that people understood and could easily relate to. In order to reach our own generation, we have to do the same thing. I have had thousands of experiences in which I have seen people in need of a touch from God. I often use the approach, "You look like you could use some encouragement. Mind if I try?" I look at the person through God's eyes, visualizing them as God sees them, not as they are today. Then I speak encouraging words to them using everyday language. How I wish someone would have done that for me years ago when I was living my life outside of a relationship with Jesus. Remember that God's kindness leads people towards repentance (Romans 2:4).

Jesus demonstrated that we should love people. It is the job of the Holy Spirit to convict people of their sin (John 16:8). Too often, we get these two turned around. Most people know their sin. What they need is someone to tell them that God loves them in spite of where they are today.

We can learn to be sensitive to people who may not know much about God and the Bible. God may then give us a word of encouragement for someone, and we can communicate it in a way that they will understand and receive what it is we are saying.

There is nothing wrong with using religious words. I love to say "Praise God!" or "Give God the glory." But there are times when it would be beneficial for the ones we are communicating with if we would use language that is more familiar to them.

To help you communicate God's love to people in need, I have listed some words commonly used by Christians that people without a religious background may not understand. Following each word are suggestions on how you might say it in regular terms. For additional help and resources on learning to speak non-religiously, visit www.dougaddison.com.

# DEFINITIONS
(CHRISTIANESE DEMYSTIFIED)

# *A*

**Anointing**
You have special characteristics. People seem to be drawn to you. You are uniquely gifted.
**Amen**
That's right! You bet! Right on! Totally!
**Assignment**
There is an evil plan against you.
**Authority**
You are a very take charge kind of person. You have clout. You are able to easily influence others. You are about to gain greater control of some situations in your life.

# *B*

**Baptism of the Holy Spirit**
New power from God. Let the Spirit fill you with God's new light and love.
**Blessing**
Good things. Something good is coming your way.
**Body of Christ**
Christians, churches. All Christians. Christians in general.
**Bondage**
Trapped or restrained.
**Born Again**
To have a spiritual awakening or spiritual experience. Turn the control of your life over to Jesus.
**Brethren**
Like-minded people. Other Christians.

## C

**Call of God**
Destiny to do something. Something you have been chosen to do.

**Calling**
What you were created to do. Something you are uniquely gifted to do.

**Chastise**
Correct or reprimand. Tell someone off.

**Check in your spirit**
Something does not sit right.

**Cleansing**
Refining, healing. Some things need to be changed. Give up some old habits.

## D

**Deliverance**
Removing any obstacles from you coming into your full destiny in God.

**Demons**
Negative forces. Something negatively influencing your life.

**Discernment**
Ability to distinguish good from evil. Able to see beneath the surface to the root of an issue.

**Disciple**
Mentor someone or become a follower of Jesus.

## E

**Edification**
Learning new things. Encouragement.

**Enemy**
Dark or negative forces. Satan.

## F

**Faith**
Trusting in what you can't see yet. Just believe. Have faith – believe that things will work out. Don't give up.

**Favor**
  Good things are coming your way.
**Flesh**
  Your own desires as opposed to what God wants for you.
**Fruit**
  As in *fruit in your life*. Character changes. Evidence of change in your life from God.
**Fruit of the Spirit**
  Good characteristics in your life from having a relationship with Jesus through the Holy Spirit.

# *G*

**Generational ties or sin**
  A negative connection through your ancestors that is blocking good things coming to you. Negative things in your family, dad or mom, grandparents, etc. that are affecting your destiny.
**Gifts**
  You have special ability. Something you are naturally good at, a God-given ability.
**Gospel**
  Message of Jesus. Good news that can help you.
**Grace**
  Things are going to be easier. Someone is going to cut you some slack.

# *H*

**Hard Ground**
  Things have been difficult for you. You have been through a lot.
**Healing**
  Things are going to change for the better. You are recovering from something.
**Heart**
  As in *I have a heart for you or getting God's heart:* I really care about you. To love someone like God does.
**Heart like David**
  You are like David of the Bible. He was small but tough and loved God.

**Holiness**
Do things right. Get it together with your spiritual life.

# I

**Intercede/Intercession**
It's more than just a quick prayer but to keep asking God to answer a prayer for someone or something.

# J-K

**Judgment**
Trouble.
**Justification**
Changed life because of Jesus dying on the cross.

# L

**Leading/Felt Led**
Directed to do. Prompted. "Felt like I should."
**Lest**
As in *lest you fall*. Better said, "or else."
**Lost**
People who don't know the love of Jesus do not like being called lost. It is better said, "Those who are not Christians," or "People who don't personally know God's love."

# M-N

**Mantle**
Something you have been created to do. You have a special purpose in life. A unique gifting, special ability from God.
**Ministry**
Something you have been chosen to do to help others, a destiny.

# O

**Old Man**
Unhealthy old habits or desires.
**On my heart**
As in *You have been on my heart*. I've been thinking about you. You have been in my thoughts.

**Open Heaven**
　　Your mind is going to get much clearer. Answers are going to come to some questions that you have.

# P

**Perseverance**
　　Stick with it even when things are hard.
**Praise**
　　Be thankful or happy.
**Pray/Prayer**
　　Meditate or meditation, reflect or reflection. Communicate with God.
**Prophecy**
　　Spiritual insight. Deeper understanding. A premonition from God.
**Prophesy**
　　To give deeper understanding. Get a message or premonition from God.
**Prophetic**
　　See and understand spiritually. Insightful, have a premonition from God.
**Purity**
　　Doing what is right. Staying away from things that may be bad for you.

# Q

**Quicken**
　　I was reminded of— Just popped into my head. I remembered.

# R

**Rapture**
　　When Jesus returns and takes people to heaven.
**Reap what you have sown**
　　Some things you have done may come back on you.
**Recompense**
　　Get what you deserve.

**Redemption**
Change for the good.
**Repent**
Ask God to forgive you and don't do it again.
**Repentant heart**
Really be sorry and ready to ask God to forgive you. Come to a place were you are really sorry for things you have done wrong.
**Resurrect**
Come to life, big-time change.
**Revelation**
New insight. Get clarity on a situation. Some questions will be answered for you.
**Righteousness**
Doing what is right.

# S

**Salvation**
Receiving forgiveness of your sins through Jesus dying on the cross. A spiritual awakening with God.
**Sanctification**
Grow spiritually. Process of allowing God to change you.
**Saved**
Spiritual. Turned the control of your life over to Jesus. Had a spiritual experience with God.
**Saved by Grace**
A new spiritual life that is not based on what we do but just because God loves us.
**Scripture**
The Bible.
**Season**
Period of time.
**Shepherd's heart**
You are a leader. You are compassionate and concerned about others.
**Sinful Nature**
Condition we are born with prior to having a spiritual awakening with God.

**Speak the truth in love**
 I need to be honest with you, but I don't want to hurt you.
**Spiritual covering**
 Mentored by someone who can help guide you spiritually.
**Spiritual gifts**
 Special characteristics. Uniqueness. You make a difference.
**Spiritual or Generational Inheritance**
 Special abilities passed down through your family.
**Steadfast**
 Stable or constant; consistency. Stay on course. Stick with it.
**Stronghold**
 Unseen obstacles that are holding you back from your destiny.
**Strongman**
 Something opposing you or holding you back.
**Stumbling block**
 Obstacles to your spiritual growth.

# T

**Tarry**
 This is a place you should linger for a while.
**Thanksgiving**
 Happy or thankful.

# U-V

**Unction**
 Compelled (by God).
**Vision**
 Clarity. See things in a different light. Seeing a picture in your mind.
**Vestibule**
 Lobby or entrance in a church.

# W

**Washed with the Blood**
 Your sins have been forgiven because of Jesus' death on the cross.
**Washing with the Word**
 Getting spiritual insight from the Bible that will help you mature spiritually.

**Wilderness**
A time when things are not very clear.
**Wisdom**
Good advice. Right thing to do, "What God may be saying to you is—"
**Witchcraft**
Negative forces. Things that are not good for you.
**Word from God**
Spiritual insight. Premonition.
**Word of God**
The Bible.
**World/Worldly**
*In the world,* not living the Christian life. *Of the world* or *worldly minded,* things that are not spiritual. Thinking in terms of physical things that are seen as opposed to God's spiritual world.

## X-Y-Z

**Zeal**
Excited or enthusiastic. You seem to have a lot of drive.

## Build Your Own Non-Relgious Vocabulary

Use the following pages to build your own list of religious words and their non-religious equivalents. Here are a few practical steps to get you started learning how to communicate without sounding religious.

1. Begin by making a list of the religious words that you say or that you hear Christians say on a regular basis. Listen for words or phrases that might be meaningless or confusing for people who don't have a church background. Use a thesaurus to find a better way to say religious-sounding words.

2. Occasionally read a modern translation of the Bible such as *The Message* or *The New Living Translation*. Look up verses that you may have memorized in a more traditional version of the Bible and note new ways to say the same thing. You'll often find fresh, inspiring ways to communicate. Make a list of phrases or ideas that you think will be understandable and inviting.

3. Get to know people outside of your Christian circles. Listen to them. You'll often discover what metaphors are meaningful to them and how they think about things from casual conversations. To communicate effectively, it's important to learn the language of the people you want to reach. Make note of common themes, ideas, or figures of speech that you notice being used.

*No More Christianese*

# Build Your Own Non-Relgious Vocabulary

*No More Christianese*

# BUILD YOUR OWN NON-RELGIOUS VOCABULARY

*No More Christianese*

# BUILD YOUR OWN NON-RELGIOUS VOCABULARY

*No More Christianese*

# BUILD YOUR OWN NON-RELGIOUS VOCABULARY